FAIRY WORLDS AND WORKERS

MW00737765

FAIRY WORLDS AND WORKERS

A natural history of fairyland

Marjorie Spock

Brush Drawings by Ingrid Gibb

& Anthroposophic Press

Copyright © 1980 by Marjorie Spock and Ingrid Gibb

Published by Anthroposophic Press

RR 4 Box 94 A1, Hudson, NY, 12534

ISBN 088010-404-X

Library of Congress Cataloging-in-Publication data is available.

10 9 8 7 6 5 4 3

All rights reserved. No part of this book may be reproduced in any form
without written permission from the publishers except for brief quotations
embodied in critical articles for reviews.

Printed in the United States of America

In memory of RUDOLF STEINER

who understood so well the living forces behind Nature

INTRODUCTION

WHEN, in the process of growing up, eternity was taken from humanity in exchange for time, human beings began feeling discontented with the earth, which came to seem a disappointing place, empty of meaning. The other, meaning-giving half of reality had somehow vanished, to become henceforth a world behind the scenes, unknowable.

For awhile people knew at least that it was there. And a few — either those who had stayed far behind the times or those who were pioneers and had advanced far ahead of them — had access to it. These reported their experience to others, and were believed or not believed, according to the hearers' make-up.

Now whenever there is something we should know about, schools are established to supply the information. The world behind the scenes was no exception. But the schools set up to teach about that world did not reach out to draw in pupils: they opened their doors only to the knock of questioners. And those who gained admittance to them were put through a training so rigorous, so demanding of changes in the neophyte, that few indeed reached initiation.

Such were the famed Mysteries of antiquity. Abydos on the Nile was an example, as were the mystery schools at Eleusis and Ephesus. Then there were the Essenes in Palestine, and the Gnostics. In the British Isles, in Brittany, and south along the coast to Asia Minor, Druids established training centers. The Middle Ages saw the rise of many schools, including those of the Knights Templar, Chartres, and the early Freemasons and Rosicrucians. Wherever the wave of culture traveled, new schools were founded.

The account given by exoteric scholarship of all these movements is misleading. All early esoteric schools were secret, in order to keep what they taught at the highest level. For this reason, present-day scholarship lacks any clue to their real nature and merely guesses at their content.

With the rise of science to cultural dominance a new challenge came to esoteric school-ing. An earlier somewhat mystical approach was largely outmoded, to be superseded by another accent: the sensitizing of an outturned gaze to perceive clairvoyantly how the World-Spirit works in matter. The veil drawn millennia before between human beings and the world behind the scenes as a result of evolutionary changes in their make-up was now to be penetrated.

At Dornach near Basel in Switzerland a modern mystery school, taught by a scientist, Dr. Rudolf Steiner, turned much of its attention to the realms of Nature and opened its doors wide to a new breed of students as interested in grasping earth as heaven.

This book owes its existence largely to what was taught and learned there about the Middle Kingdom and its beings.

* * *

That fairyland and its denizens should be as much a concern of scientists as they have long been of poets and painters and storytellers was one of Steiner's deep convictions. For he was a close observer of their life and work, and it was clear to him that they were of profound importance to the earth. He saw in them Nature's servitors, beings charged not only with the maintenance of Nature's household but with her evolutionary plans as well. In his view, fairy tales in which these beings figured were not mere literature but accounts of subtler layers of fact, clothed in poetic imagery. And he spoke repeatedly of the vital need to recognize the fairies' work and to prize them, since only so could their efforts prosper and the earth be carried forward in its evolution.

That Steiner himself knew and loved the Little People no one could doubt who heard him describe them. At such times his hearers were transported straight into the atmosphere of fairyland, feeling its magic. And from that time forward they looked upon Nature with a different gaze. The veil obscuring the intense life and consciousness behind it was drawn aside, and they saw it peopled as we shall try to show it in what follows.

* * *

CLOSE ENOUGH TO TOUCH with an outstretched hand or the mere lifting of an eyebrow lie the borders of a fabulous country. It was once familiar ground to all, a place where gods and men lived together in profound communion. But new goldfields of experience beckoned; the old was abandoned in a rush, lost sight of, and soon largely forgotten. Now people are beginning to feel bereft without it and are trying to find their way back again to that lost kingdom.

Various times and races gave it different names. To some it was Paradise, to others Tir-nan-Og; Arthurian Avalon; the Country underneath the Sea; Fairyland; the World of Immortal Youth; the Land of Heart's Desire. These are but a few of its past designations. In speaking it here we shall call it, for reasons that will immediately appear, the Middle Kingdom.

Where, exactly is that country? and what is it in the middle of?

Well, if God's is the world of creative *power* and ours the world of created *objects*, the Middle Kingdom is the land of *life* that lies between them, serving as the bridge for their interaction. It extends wherever vital processes are going on: upward into sunlight and the warmth-realm called the troposphere, sidewise with the spreading flow of water, downward into the dark depths of earth where roots grow and veins of metal run.

It is easy to see how the land of life came to be thought of as the Land of Heart's Desire. Is not life the most prized possession of all living creatures? and inner aliveness the most sought-after good? Does it not instantly put to flight those bugbears boredom, heaviness, and gloom? Do not the aspects of life, physical and spiritual, always wear the glow of magic emanating from life's power to quicken? Yes, life can be observed to cast enchantment on every single thing it touches. And whatever it touches blossoms, moreover, into beauty.

Now the Middle Kingdom has as its native population innumerable hosts of fairies. They are by no means the only dwellers there. But they form the Middle Kingdom workforce, whose function it is to convey life through the realms of Nature. Four races of Little People (as tradition also calls the fairies) serve the four elements: earth, air, fire and water. Gnomes are the caretakers of the earth-realm, undines or water-spirits wielders of fluids, Sylphs rule the element of light and air. Fire-spirits reign over processes of heat.

But it would be a mistake to picture the Little People carrying on their work in a do-gooding spirit. Virtue does not interest fairies; it would scarcely occur to them that they "serve" Nature. Nor are they purposeful in their activity, singling out tasks to perform and then setting about them. They simply react to their environment in love or loathing. For they are ruled exclusively by feeling—feeling more intense by far than any familiar to most human beings.

Of the many kinds of places they frequent, fairies of all four races are most drawn to forests. This is because of the intense life concentrated in them. Is not each single tree among the multitude a burgeoning garden? a garden raised from the horizontal to the vertical, its trunk a seedbed for the growth of branches, each branch in turn a further ground from which sprout countless twigs with leaves and flowers? No other earthly area so teems with vigor.

But fairies have even better reasons for their love of forests. Not a tree but reminds them of the World Tree, Igdrasil, the great Tree of Life, which—Nordic legend tells us—grows at the heart of fairyland and with fairy help draws the sap of heaven down to course in every living thing of earth. To the Little People every tree, no matter how small, lopsided or scrawny it may be, is a loved offspring of the Tree of Life. This attracts fairies to places on the earth where trees throng together. It may also explain why we human beings feel such awe on entering a forest. Every tiniest clump of trees has the aura of an enchanted wood about it, for it is magical with life, and fairies dwell there.

No wonder the ancients established sacred groves wherein to worship, feeling themselves closely akin there to the realm of spirits! No wonder people of our own time are always likening forests to cathedrals!

* * *

The four races of fairies are by no means limited to one particular story in Nature's four-tiered dwelling. Quite the opposite: the liveliest exchange takes place up and down as the various groups go about their business, which is to serve life and its evolution. Indeed, without such interaction there could be no life.

But before considering how they interact, let us observe how each race of the Little People lives and works in its own element.

*　　*　　*

Since gnomes and human beings are alike earthbound creatures, we will probably find gnomes—or cobolds, or goblins, as they are sometimes also called—the fairy race closest to our understanding.

Their habitat is one few other forms of life would care for, for gnomes live down below the surface of our planet, where roots take an anchor-hold on earth. If you should chance to wonder how any creature other than a worm gets about through a medium so dense you need only consider how easily thoughts pass through the hard heads of human beings and you will at once understand the matter. Thoughts are not of flesh, though they must live in it for us to know them, and neither are fairies.

Gnomes are immensely clever Little People, with large heads out of all proportion to their tiny bodies. Fairy tales tell how they carry lamps to light them on their subterranean wanderings. This is, of course, just a way of speaking, for the light cast is not an outer brightness, but rather inner light, shed on the nature of what they find about them by their keen intelligence. They have what we might call a "knowing eye," which understands at a glance everything it falls on. They do not need to go through a laborious process of "figuring things out." To see a human being puzzling to solve a problem prompts them to make rather rude remarks. "What fools these mortals be!" is, I'm afraid, only too typical of their attitude. They constantly admonish us, "O Human, awaken!" For to them anyone who has to think to get at facts is half asleep. Indeed, they consider thinking as we know it just a means of pulling oneself together from a bout of dreaming. Since they are wide awake already, they perceive what is without having to mull it over in their heads.

Gnomes are the only beings in the world who never sleep. This is because they are afraid to do so. They believe that any slackening of attention forebodes double tragedy: the dissolution of their bodies (which they rightly or wrongly feel must be held together by sheer concentration) and the frightful disgrace of being ignorant of what goes on. This characteristic of gnomes has given rise to an admonition often heard by Central European children: "Wake up and pay attention like a gnome!"

There could be no such things as plant or tree roots if there were no gnomes to tend their development. Gnomes are at work all through the year marshalling mineral nutrients around them and wielding magnetic forces to draw them down to a firm grounding in the earth.

Gnomes are born old; the years weigh on them. Not that they suffer from the crotchets of old age; they are merry little beings, with a love of fun. But when they journey from beneath earth's surface to some fairy ring in a forest clearing they do not take part in any dancing that goes on there, but merely sit and watch, making old-man jokes and comments on the dancers. As the ancients they are, they would feel it beneath their dignity to toss their limbs about in lighthearted abandon as the younger elves do.

Tradition has been prone to picture gnomes as wizened little old men with bent backs and knobby, spindly limbs. There is more truth than fiction in this portraiture, for gnomes are a very ancient race, tiny in comparison with human beings (dozens can come packed in a rock like sardines in tins), and do indeed gravitate to dryness both in their surroundings and their sense of humor. They shrink from the damp cold of the earth they work in and from the chill creatures that inhabit it — *most particularly frogs*, which, being the antithesis of gnomes, fill them with loathing. Frogs are invariably pompous natures, something no gnome could ever let himself become. They are, moreover, rather formless organisms, soft, squashy, bulbous all over, whereas gnomes are sharply distinct of form, built in mind and body on the principle of spareness. This tends to make gnomes beings "of few words," and those words pithy. Frogs, quite the opposite, are garrulous, and, like garrulous natures wherever we find them, given to utterances of no startling significance; they drive gnomes distracted with the endless repetition of their mindless chant. Isn't it sad that the cheery harrumphing that sounds from wet places on spring and summer nights should strike so disagreeably on the ears of gnomes that these otherwise sensible beings shudder when they hear it! Even the thrilling note of the "spring peeper," *hyla crucifer*, lacks power to charm.

Gnomes detest frogs for a further reason: they see in them creatures they might themselves become were they to fail even for a moment to maintain the sharp vigilance that belongs to gnomehood. Never yet has a gnome been transformed into a frog. But so neurotic are they on this subject that you could not persuade a single one of them that such a fate may not overhang him.

The moon, that tide-and-rain-related planet, is equally anathema to gnomes, who regard it as the creator and ruler of the watery element. They cannot bear its rays upon their bodies. When the moon fulls, flooding all the world with its soft light-ocean, gnomes so harden their exteriors against it that they go about on the surface of the earth looking like tiny knights in suits of armor.

But they have pleasures too, incomparable ones, which certainly outweigh any suffering they may have to endure at the hands of moisture. These little beings, from tip to toe one tingling sensor, have as their own special fairyland the subterranean realm of metals and crystals, through which they wander tasting all manner of delight in its transit. Mortals see that realm only as a finished world, still, hard and unchanging, hence possessing a deathlike quality. But to the gnomes' subtle sensing it is all alive, a world of moving forces rather than of matter, still endowed with the music and colorfulness of its cosmic origin. And we mortals can share this experience in part if we are fortunate enough to witness a melting-down or, more accurately put, a melting-*up* of metals. For this is a process wherein heat frees metals from the solid state and returns them to the flowing and then aeriform condition in which they existed when the world was young and they had but lately issued from primeval fire. Crystals have, of course, kept material reminiscences of their primal color. And to guess at the music imprisoned in them we have only to recall the crystal-like figures produced by musical vibrations and first discovered by Chladnius. Geometric form is always frozen music!

But gnomes have still more incomparable joys. They are the *knowers* among elementals. As such they possess a strong affinity to inner light (indeed, their very bodies are formed of the light-stuff of intelligence). So it has naturally fallen to their lot to receive a special gift of insight: *the ability to see ideas as we see objects*. The whole world of creative thought lies open to their observation. They behold the working of the minds of God and men as these are inspired to bring into being some new form of life — whether it take shape as a spiral nebula, a new species of plant or animal, the geodesic dome, Shelley's *Ode to a Skylark*, Brahms's *Lullaby*, a piece of philosophic insight, or countless other inspirations fully as worthy of being mentioned. Nor do gnomes fritter away this endowment "putting two and two together" to come out with trivial bits of understanding. Rather do they use their love of knowing as a magnet to draw down to themselves and thus ground in our planet the shaping thoughts that flow into evolution from the mind of God. It can scarcely be a negligible experience to be made thus privy to divine imagining!

And how are these visions carried to their destination in the souls of gnomes?

Why, they are conveyed to plants in light-rays, and plants serve as their further conduits into earth.

It is no more astounding, when you stop to think about it, that God should convey His ideas to gnomes using the medium of plants than that we should transmit ours to friends at a distance by means of an electric current running through cables. And do we not do exactly as God does and "say it with flowers" when we have things too deep for words to communicate?

We too can share with gnomes this wealth of heaven, this treasure of divine creative visions. But lest in our unreadiness it overwhelm us, gnomes translate these mighty generative ideas into symbols, the miniature images of fairy stories, and pass them on in this more easily assimilable state to human beings.

Elizabeth Barrett Browning perfectly expressed the truth that the great can be discovered in the small by seeing eyes when she wrote that

> ....Nothing's small;
> ...No pebble at your feet but proves a sphere;
> No chaffinch but implies the cherubim;
> Earth's crammed with heaven,
> and every common bush afire with God.
> But only he who sees takes off his shoes,
> The rest sit round it and pluck blackberries.

There may nevertheless be readers disinclined to attribute tales like Snow White, the Frog Prince or Sleeping Beauty to so high an origin. Let them explain, then, how it came about that the myths and legends and fairy tales of widely separated times and places bear so strong a family resemblance, remain so ageless, and possess such quickening and imperishable life. And let it be remembered that these tales did not begin life as children's entertainment, but as Literature, deserving of the capital L we have given it. Though nowadays it is chiefly children, themselves fresh from the realm of cosmic life and doubtless missing it, who are enthralled by and seek out fairy tales as nourishment.

Now gnomes will not part with their fairy-tale treasures to just anybody, even supposing the would-be listener speaks their language. Enticement is necessary, a trade indicated. They will welcome you into their midst and match you story for story if you can narrate to them the carryings-on of babies, those droll and fascinating human spirits who, because they are still so untouched by earthiness, remain as invisible to gnomes as gnomes to us.

It may strike some reading this account that gnomes are not very social natures. And they are right: these Little People are marked individualists, strongly ruled by antipathy. Their dryness is a separating factor; it takes water — or, rather, the undines who rule that element — to join things together. Gnomes do not even take much interest in their fellow gnomes. But perhaps low-level sociability is not to be expected in the case of beings whose minds are given over to divine ideas. Then too, did you ever know anybody with a sharp nose, sharp eyes and a sharp intelligence who overflowed with kindly feeling? Such temperaments grow easily exasperated, as wide-awake souls cannot help but do when confronted with the vagueness of the half-asleep. If gnomes play tricks upon us when we stumble about in this condition — and they love to! — it is out of a natural desire to wake us up. It is they who steer heedless feet to the stones we stub our toes on, they who betray us into the phrase that makes an unforgettable faux pas, they who jog the drowsy hand that spills the milk.

No malicious intent underlies these actions; gnomes are merely trying to rouse us from habitual dreaming, to make us as aware as they are. Since this is one of the tasks assigned them, it would spell delinquency on their part to miss such good chances to startle us awake.

Their love of fun prompts gnomes to be great entertainers. When they befriend human beings gnomes like to enact little dramas to amuse them. An acquaintance of the writer, packing up for a visit to a goatkeeper, observed a group of gnomes in her cottage merrily stuffing tiny goatskin costumes into infinitesimal red luggage. On another occasion the same acquaintance woke one morning to see, standing by her bedside looking at her with a twinkling eye, a creature which she at first mistook for her pet pheasant from the woods outside. She was wondering sleepily how the bird had managed to get in when she noticed something strange about it: instead of the single tuft of feathers, running front to back, which adorns the heads of normal pheasants, this one had two tufts, arching sidewise. The pheasant vanished into thin air as she saw through the spoof.

Another friend, playing a game of Mah Jong, carelessly jostled the table, spilling tiles onto the floor. No amount of searching led to their recovery. As the players were cutting paper pieces to replace them, the lost tiles clattered back onto the table from the air above it.

Episodes of this sort, where objects disappear and work or play is annoyingly halted, are rather frequent occurrences, so much so that people have coined a term for the disrupters: gremlins.

But gnomes make pleasant friends for the most part. You can attach them to yourself much as you would attract a bird or squirrel or any other creature of the forest: first, by becoming aware of their existence, and then offering them a treat. In the gnomes' case a pineapple is the appropriate bait, for they are drawn to this fruit like iron filings to a magnet. Not that they eat it; it is simply a focus of heart's interest to them, in the sense that a beautiful view or the fragrance of a rose delights human beings. Its mere presence suffices to intrigue them.

One can also get to know them by becoming a miner, though that would be a hard price to pay for the privilege when there are so much more attractive ways to do it, such as training oneself to be wide awake. But in the old pick-and-shovel days many a miner witnessed the little fellows leaping free of the rock he was breaking up, and he carried on conversations with them.

*   *   *

Undines

Gnomes

Fire-Spirits

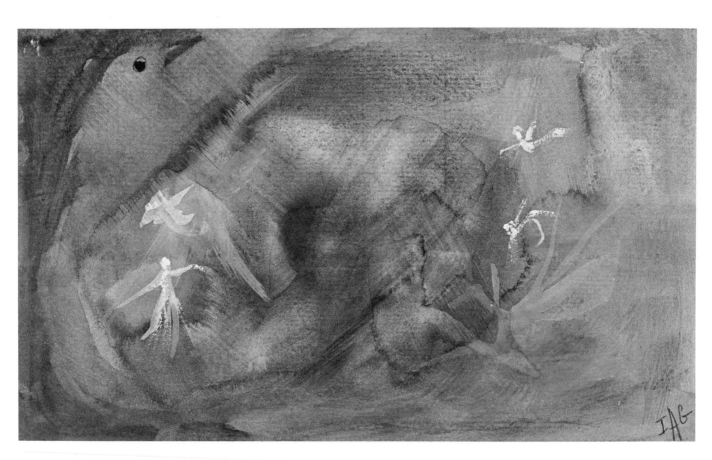

Sylphs

What a giant step must be taken by one who, after looking in on gnomes in their subterranean habitat, sets out to visit undines on the floor above! It is not a simple matter of walking upstairs. One has to make a deliberate change, a shift from thinking to feeling, from crystallinity to metamorphic flow. One has, in short, to abandon the sharp focus of the waking state and melt over consciously into the liquidity of dreaming. For that is how it feels to be an undine. This group is the elemental kingdom meant to dream.

Water — or, more accurately, the fluid element — presents a soul-like picturing of undine inwardness. Is water not dream-stuff par excellence? Are creatures swimming in it not suspended, horizontal as in sleeping, in dream-buoyancy? Water has no sharp edges to come up against, no impenetrable barriers such as elsewhere shock into awakening those colliding with them. Its very transparency is dreamlike. Looking through water on a still, dark day, or in shadowy places where there is no glitter on its surface, one can feel uncertain whether it is even there. At such times it appears "as insubstantial as a dream."

So we may picture undines floating all a-dream in a sea of images, a sea which is both their inner and their outer world — for like water, they know no hard and fast divisions. It is their nature, just as it is water's, to commingle, to combine with and seep into everything about them. Their dreaming, like all dreaming, streams in a process of eternal change. We human beings, predestined by our belonging to the earth to form fixed concepts, can hardly conceive of an inwardness so mobile, one that flows through form that is also in flux and never comes to rest within static limits. We call this process metamorphosis, the law of life that rules emergent evolution.

Undines may thus be thought of as the great transformers; they are the chemists of the elemental world. It is undines who, in accordance with their inner life, and using fluids as their medium, cause substances to intermingle and undergo the process known as chemical change.

To catch sight of undines you must go where water and air mix and commingle. Undines are all flowing motion, streaming shapes never twice the same. And when veils of rain sweep over a landscape and mist rises to drift over hills and valleys, there you will find these willowy dreamers playing in the metamorphosis of form, trailing about in shifting cloud masses.

But undines too have a task assigned them. It is they who draw sap, the clear life-blood of vegetation, up the trunks of trees and stems of plants to join forces with the light in foliage; they who bring about change in the shape and composition of substances as they wield the fluid element to bind and loosen.

This they do — under the inspiration of their dreaming — by means of the life-force inherent in rhythm, an always magical power given into their keeping by the goddess Nature. They set innumerable little tides in motion, governing their rise and fall, their welling up and ebbing. And in this slow and graceful dancing they weave flowing patterns into the living robe of the goddess, shapes that come into being and dissolve again: cloud and mist forms; leaves put forth at intervals alternating with the contraction of a plant stem; trains of vortices in water streaming. For undines are presto-change-o artists who, delighting in variety, keep the material world in flux as they live out in rhythm the shaping impulses born of their creative dreaming.

Undines, however, are not proper earthlings in the sense of clinging to "life" as do humans and animals. Dreaming being kin to sleep and sleep to dying, they are already partly loosened and dreaming of release from bondage to any tasks related to matter. Even the median realm of rhythm where they work, tending the rise and fall of sap, bringing about material comminglings, joining with sylphs to set on foliage, taking part with them in the ups and downs of weather patterns, is one where they feel tied to earthly servitude. They yearn to escape, to "die" and return to their cosmic origin.

Little of the separatist tendency, the splitting apart into isolated units that is so characteristic of the earthy element, is encountered in undines. The way of water is to join together, to overcome separateness; it may be called the social force among the four elements. This is due, of course, to the sociality of undines, whose nature water faithfully reflects. You will scarcely — if ever — come upon a water-sprite working alone; cooperation is their strong point. They reach out not only to each other but almost equally to sylphs, for these share the realm of rhythm with them.

There is one area, however, in which little remains of their sympathetic feeling. When, in the ceaseless flow of form to which they are subject, they approach the fish-shape, which we think so graceful, shivers of revulsion shake them, and they hurry through it with all the despatch of which their dreaming natures are capable.

Just as gnomes are caretakers of the earthy element and undines of water, sylphs — the spirits of the light-filled air — do their work in the atmosphere, darting about in the wake of birds, whose flight, to their ears, makes music on the air-waves. Sylphs live in a world of tone, a realm of sounding glitter so vivid that even human ears and eyes catch glimpses of it. This is evident in our use of such terms as "color-tone" and "tone-coloring," which indicate that in some deeper level of our being we are dimly aware of the fairy world behind what we are wont to call reality. We seem to sense that in a fuller experience color can be heard and music seen.

Is there a lovelier word than "sylph" in any language? Must we not have been inspired when we gave this name to the lissome beings of the light and air? Every letter in it conjures up a picture of their souls and motion. "S" suggests their silvery-scintillating sparkle, the swiftness and suddenness with which they soar or swoop or swirl or speed away, the songlike sounding of their passage; "Y" (as in short "I") their arrowy darting; "L" their lift and lilt, their liveliness, their light, their loving natures; "Ph" ("F") the flash, the flare-up, the flitting, the firefly flickering with which they suddenly appear or disappear.

Imagine the air latticed with the glittering, streaking paths of these small meteors. And then contrast with this the vaporlike slow wafting and watery undulating of the undines and the stalwart stance of gnomes standing at the roots of plants raptly contemplating the descent of God's ideas. Some invisible frontier which divides the upper from the lower elements, the free from the earthbound, has been crossed here. And this applies to the inner scene as well, for the souls of sylphs and fire-spirits know no aversion such as that felt by gnomes in relation to frogs and by undines at the sight of fishes; rather are their attitudes toward everything in Nature wholly sympathetic.

Sylphs work in closest communion with the undines, with whom they are wielders of the magic power of rhythm. They bring the creative forces of the light-world to commingle with the flow of sap in vegetative greening and in the taking on of blossom color. Acting together in dancelike interchange, sylphs and undines weave the endlessly varied fabric of the weather.

Birds are the special love of sylphdom. Indeed, a sylph passing through a birdless area such as a city street unlined with trees and lacking any such vegetative life as that induced to sprout in window boxes feels itself woefully incomplete; it suffers from a kind of sylph-amnesia which only the presence of a bird can cure. Selfhood thus comes to sylphs from outside themselves; it does not spring up within them as with us. They sense themselves rather as enclosed in blessing than as possessors of an inner center. Self-experience, with them, can therefore never be tainted with self-centeredness. This fits them to take on the selfless mission of serving as carriers of love through Nature.

Sylphs perform as vital services for birds as birds for sylphs. It is sylphs, at home in the tone-filled realm of air, who teach baby birds to sing and fly and who play a guiding role in bird migrations. The next time you look up at a flock traveling northward or southward with the changing seasons you might try to listen in as with a sylph's ears to the multicolored sounding of its passage. At such times the sky overhead becomes a mighty windharp, the air a kaleidoscope of rainbow tone.

Bees hold almost as strong an attraction for the sylphs as birds do. When they are about their work of gathering nectar, a miniature bright aura of delight surrounds them, and sylphs are drawn to it as by a magnet. Flowerbeds where bees vie with hummingbirds for honey offer unmatched opportunity to observe sylphs in a setting where the auric rainbows that encircle bees make a second glowing garden in the midst of blossoms.

But sylphs are found most busily at work wherever in Nature a checking, an ebbing of the first floodtide of life signals the onset of maturity, a crossing over to the blossoming, fruiting stage. Is not this quite in accord with the mission of sylphs as carriers of love? For what is love, in any kingdom or on any level, if not blossoming, maturing, fruiting? In love's higher forms even the selflessness of sylphs is present!

* * *

The outermost ring of the terrestrial globe which is Nature's home-away-from-home (for, be it remembered, she is a goddess and only comes to earth to work here) is the troposphere. It is the realm ruled over by fire-spirits, the fairy race closest to the cosmic source of things. They are the beings on whose wings warmth is brought into our planet.

Not that they create warmth; their task is rather to imbue it with life, life drawn from the wellsprings of the Middle Kingdom, so that it can be assimilated by all living things.

In the vegetative world, fire-spirits join forces with sylphs at a certain stage of plant maturing, adding the element of cosmic warmth to the cosmic love and light sylphs bring to Nature. Pollen dust is the material means, the miniature aircraft, whereby fire-spirits carry warmth to its destination. In this connection it may be of interest to recall that when Piccard, the pioneer balloonist, entered the troposphere, he was nonplussed to find himself travelling through clouds of pollen.

Bees are no less beloved by fire-spirits than by sylphs; indeed, all insects that play a part in pollination are their cherished fellow workers and companions. The same extraordinarily brilliant aura clothes them. Clairvoyant sight discovers this to be the fire-spirit that accompanies every such insect on its pollinating rounds.

But the creature dear to them above all others is the butterfly. What birds are to sylphs, butterflies are to fire-spirits: givers of the gift of selfhood. Sylphs, however, merely need to see a bird to feel complete, whereas fire-spirits achieve this only in innermost union with their counterparts.

Fire-spirits are the generative force serving Nature, ensuring the on-goingness of species. They are the winged messengers who bring from on high the formative ideas which sylphs and gnomes and undines body forth in plant and animal evolution. Can the means to this: seeds — infinitesimal specks of matter that they are — be recognized as anything more than "X marks the spot" where such living thought-forms await springtime resurrection? How many mortals suspect the presence of a flame of life already burning in these tiny vessels?

It must be clear to any thoughtful mind that seeds carry the signature of fire-spirits, for they are the storage-place in plants of oils, a flammable element.

Were it not for the fact that warmth or fire, the province of fire-spirits, is such a common phenomenon, witnessed every time we light a match, we should hardly be able to contain our wonder at the properties of this element. They account for the appeal of a wood fire, before which we are almost irresistibly drawn to linger, watching flames spring in and out of being as though conjured forth by the machinations of a skilled magician.

But one who not only shares this pleasure but becomes a student of what fire can teach finds that it offers a front row seat at ever fresh enactments of the world's First Day. One can observe here how warmth, a purely spiritual energy, moving into the beginning figure of the dance of life, undergoes miraculous transformation into outer substance, the ephemeral materiality of flame.

There can be no more potent quickener than this "baptism of fire," no more ideal conditioning to attune oneself to the life-realm of the Middle Kingdom.

Fire-spirits are among the first we learn to see there. And as our world was once born of fire and every true idea is still begotten in the warm glow of enthusiasm, so fire-spirits will be found wielding that primeval element, mothering summer's heat around the swelling fruits, sweetening, bringing them to ripeness, letting us taste and smell the sun and planets in their savors. They bring seeds, those tiny clinkers of their burning, to maturity. And from their hands the dreams of next year's vegetation fall with the seed to earth for gnomes to nourish; henceforth the underworld is warmed and lit, as our inner world is, with visions, the cherished images of things-to-be that fuel evolution.

So the wheel turns, the cycle rounds from fulfillment to a new beginning.

Thus far no mention has been made of the wicked fairies whose evil-doing adds so much drama to certain fairy stories. But there are such in every race of elementals. They are small but by no means harmless servitors of Lucifer and Satan, underlings who take the same delight as do these fallen angels in denaturing Nature and turning balance topsy-turvy. And we human beings bring them new recruits when we fail to give the Little People recognition.

It is not a case of fairies resembling children who demand attention from the grownups and throw horrid tantrums when it is withheld. Elementals are the living soul of Nature; they do the work that "makes the world go 'round"—the living world. And it is not a matter of small consequence whether we see and know this and do all we can to support their activity or whether we hinder it by treating Nature as a mere machine to be exploited, tinkered with, and changed at will. Fairies have needs which we must satisfy if they are to work well. But of this below.

So we find wicked gnomes, undines, sylphs, and fire-spirits, all wreaking devastation in their element wherever things get out of balance. They are in earthquakes, landslides, crumblings; in water on the rampage. They ride the whirlwind in cyclones, hurricanes, typhoons, tornadoes. They summon up volcanoes from earth's depths and call down light-nings. They are behind freezing cold and searing heat. They provide the sting or poison to every stinging, poisonous plant or animal. And they invade human nature when we lose inner balance, pushing us to excesses or one-sidedness: gnomes, when our thinking shrivels to cold logic; undines, when feeling overflows its bounds; sylphs, when wills turn fanatical; fire-spirits, when selfhood allows itself to become puffed up into self-importance.

* * *

The Middle Kingdom has been referred to as the *Land of Life*, that part of the universe from which life issues. It was further described as the realm mediating between earth and heaven. For it is in the Middle Kingdom that God's ideas, making their way to embodi-ment in matter, are clothed about with the life-forces needed to sustain them.

The beings who do this clothing and sustaining are the fairies. In view of the impor-tance of their work we must take care, when we call them Little People, to do so cherish-ingly, looking up, not down. Small of stature they may be. But what would become of the earth—and of ourselves — if they were to vanish? Without gnomes there would be no solid ground to stand on, no firm bones to make a scaffolding inside us and the animals, no logical structure in our thinking; without undines no life-giving lakes and streams and oceans to lave the dry land, no green vegetation, no circulating fluids in our bodies, no liquid world of feeling in our souls; without sylphs no movement of air nor blessing of the light, no flowers, no purposeful wills; without fire-spirits no warmth, no hearths to sit by, no fruits or fragrances or grains, no fire-core of selfhood. For all this, and a great deal more, we owe the fairies thanks and recognition. It is they who keep the earth so alive that the elements, their provinces, are faithful outpicturings of the soul of Nature. Our whole world lives in soul and body because of the presence of the Little People in it.

In olden times people knew a thing or two we have forgotten. They saw and worshipped Nature as a goddess. There was no question in their minds but that the living world was fairy country, where dwelt an infinitude of lesser spirits over whom she reigned. Natural events were regarded as their acts, performed in her service. And from every tree, every cloud, every spring, every flower these beings spoke with a voice to which the people hearkened. For wisdom is the breath of life in Nature, the exhalation of the goddess, and it was this wisdom that they sought in listening.

So it was from the Little People that human beings of earlier times learned such things as the secrets of the healing powers of plants, the properties of metals, the care of fields and flocks and crops and children, life's wise management.

Under such circumstances human beings and Nature were one heart and soul, and fairies the mouthpiece through which they communicated.

Nature today is still of the stature of a goddess. She still reigns over the Middle Kingdom, is still served by the Little People, still infuses all the world of life with wisdom. But the human race has largely broken its earlier close connection with her. We have been staring so hard at the material world, intent on deciphering its composition, that we have lamed our power of vision for the soul behind it.

The tide is beginning to turn again, however. We miss the magical realm of creative beings which is at least half — and the more important half — of reality. Then too, wisdom has come to be in short supply as we deal practically with Nature, and there is little left to call on. The problems this causes are overwhelming; we are beginning to be frightened into looking deeper.

This will prove to be a great adventure. For if we look deep enough to solve them we will find ourselves across the border between the world of matter and the Middle Kingdom, entering into renewed communion with the fairies.

*   *   *

The key that unlocks the door to fairyland is liveliness of spirit. It is available to everybody. But like many a key in long disuse it has grown rusty and usually needs quite a bit of polishing to make it work.

Now everyone knows without having to be told so that life, wherever met with in its pristine state wears an aura that is purest magic. Think, for instance, of a fresh spring morning; of mountain air; of kittens playing, or lambs or kids cavorting in a meadow; of the call of a woodthrush breaking the silence of a forest; of being in love.

Nor do natural events like these exhaust the possibilities of magic. There is the life of human spirits which has poured forth such an incalculable wealth of beauty and meaning, and continues to do so. It has only to touch prisoners of the mundane with its magic wand to free them for the moment into realms of experience where they become tinglingly alive. Everyone must recall occasions when a lively piece of music, for example, quickened the hearers, making their eyes dance, setting their hands to clapping and their feet to tapping, lifting their hearts, opening vistas — however nebulous and fleeting — into a vividness of which their everyday awareness knows nothing. The music has transferred its life to them.

There is always this mysterious contagion in the lively; it is more catching than the measles. And few, very few, ever develop an immunity to it. In fact, the opposite is true: each further exposure tends to make us more susceptible.

It need not be a matter of happenstance whether one falls heir to the natural and spiritual life that abounds around us. Rather is it a question of letting ourselves realize that it is there, and then of seizing every opportunity to live it.

That we so often fail to see and seize these opportunities is what drives gnomes to their despairing cry, "O Human, awaken!"

If you were to seek advice from gnomes as to how to go about this awakening they would tell you, "It is very simple: just pay attention to differences."

They love, of course, to be enigmatic. What subtle mind ever contents itself with a plain answer?

So this one, too, like others they give, requires a little living into. If one takes it to heart — and that is where it must be taken — one finds that they are really saying that everything is a mystery until one discovers and can pinpoint its uniqueness. And that stands out most strikingly where there is contrast. Would we, for example, feel the qualities of light so poignantly if there were no darkness to offset it? What would we understand of winter without summer, of spring without autumn? of cold without heat? of sound without silence? of stillness if there were no such thing as motion? of water were it not for the hard earth, the circling air, consuming fire?

One begins to grasp that the first thing the gnomes want to have us see is the polar structure of the universe, wherein contrasts lie. An awakening experience indeed, to arrive at insight into the design of Nature, to perceive the scaffolding whereon the world is built! May we not call this most significant reality?

But further stages of awakening beckon; we need not stop at perceiving polarities. For the poles from which differences spring are dynamic entities, every one of which is doing something. And when they work with or on each other, the border areas thus created become the scene of happenings of uncommon interest, the dramatic locus "where the action is," the birthplace of life. Think of the commotion that sets in when fire and water come together! Think of the color that is born when light strikes into darkness or darkness overpowers light!

Scientists have coined the dry term "interfaces" for these borders. This repels gnomes, who believe with the poet Novalis that "the more poetical, the truer," and therefore always employ fairytale imagery to describe a fact. They call all such places thresholds, where doors open into the Land of Life, the Middle Kingdom. And they see thresholds everywhere, frontier upon frontier, each one a crossing point into fuller experience, each a fuller opportunity for waking.

We humans may not as yet be very wide awake. But deep down we do have some measure of awareness, some sensitive feeling for differences and thresholds such as the gnomes are urging us to sharpen. Who, for example, does not know the fascination of a shoreline and expect to discover who-knows-what there besides a meeting place of land and water? Would anyone be very much surprised to catch a fleeting glimpse of fairies among the bees laboring in a flower garden? What palpable magic surrounds outcroppings of ledge with patches of moss or lichens growing on them! Is not half the joy of boating, the experience of moving on a surface where light glitters on the water, winds stir up waves, and there is the seen and known above us, mystery below? Why are we touched by the sight of cattle grazing in green meadows or lying in a rocky pasture? What do we find so enlivening about wind rippling through a grain field? Why do we feel, entering a clearing in the forest, that we have stumbled upon fairy country? And why is the heart stirred when we witness devotion and understanding between a human being and an animal? We feel, we know that much more is taking place at all these borders than our physical senses are capable of registering, and we respond, quickened, to its stimulus.

*   *   *

It is no easy feat for people of our time to see the fairies. Yet there are four professions which offer their practitioners unique opportunities to know them. Farmers, fishermen, foresters and miners work not just at the threshold of fairyland but well inside it, in the heart of Nature where the Little People carry on their labors. So the miner delves in earth's rocky fastness where gnomes dwell and are constantly encountered. The forester or lumberjack spends daylight hours deep in woodland glades among gnomes and undines. The fisherman, abroad upon the waters, surrounded by fogs and spray and heaving billows, has undines all about, sylphs above. And who but the farmer toils in open country where all four fairy races do their work, sharing the care of fields and soil and crops and animals?

Must not the very nature of their enterprise condition such people to sense the presence of these unseen helpers and open themselves to them—even if unconsciously—to fairy tutelage? What if they describe as "hunches" the insight they glean from companioning elementals? Do not those who work thus close to Nature often strike us as curiously knowledgeable, and not just about concerns of their professions? The goddess makes them wise, as a child is, or a fairy.

Of all four professions the farmer's is the most privileged. People think of this life as dull and narrow. But how could it be either? What is narrow about a life lived in the open between earth and sky? or dull when the person living it can observe the happenings in both these regions of the universe and hourly witness the tremendous drama of their interplay? Farmers enjoy front row seats at ever freshly enacted miracles of growth; the world is in movement all about them. How then could they know and be oppressed by the stagnation, the heaviness of spirit that so frequently weighs down the city dweller?

The farmer's whole concern is with the living, constantly studying how it may be enhanced. Insightful farmers even learn to transform dead wastes into life by composting, mixing this quickened substance with their soil like bakers stirring yeast into their bread dough. Fairies are strongly attracted by this practice. They swarm to the farmer's aid, and the farm prospers.

Taught by Rudolf Steiner, the biodynamic farmer adds a further lure. Four kinds of sprays are readied as enticements and spread in, on or above the fields at the proper seasons. To strengthen gnome activity in roots a spray made of treated cow manure is used (for gnomes and cows have a special affinity) and dug into the soil at planting. A spray of stinging nettle — nectar to undines — is applied when the sap runs, stalks shoot, and the first leaves begin unfolding their green petals. When the second set of leaves appears, sylphs are attracted by a spray of quartz made of crystals finely ground and activated, then loosed into the air above the fields as a sparkling vapor. This spray is also used after dark, wet weather to magnify sunlight and heighten chlorophyll production. Lastly, at the blossoming and fruiting stage, warmth is intensified and chilling averted by spraying a tea prepared from valerian, an offering to which fire-spirits swarm as bees to honey.

A farm where such practices are followed is one where human beings are in league with Nature. It becomes part of the Land of Life, the Middle Kingdom. The soil teems with activity, plants thrive, animals prosper. Fairies abound there. And farmers whose intuition is open to their guidance may one day find their eyes opening too and begin to see the Little People working along with them.

*   *   *

It is wise, on encountering a fairy, not to be too overeager in one's scrutiny. Little People — like those other innocents, animals, and children — have an intense dislike of being stared at. They love to stare at us, of course, but will turn away at once and disappear the moment we return the favor. They have grown shy in the face of our disbelief in them. Then too, they lack the assurance, born of selfhood, that can stand up under the searching eyes of other selves. So one has to cultivate "second sight," that way of looking which perceives things subtly, as though with an inner, sidewise glance. Then we feel their life so keenly as to see it.

To feel life: that is the key to acquaintance with the Little People and to their land of life, the Middle Kingdom.

But a further threshold lies beyond, which, if we cross it, leads to re-acquaintance with the goddess Nature, bringing us in touch again with wisdom. That is a step on which much hangs. Fairies delight in teaching us to take it, and they love to accompany us into the presence of their goddess.

Paying attention to differences, noting thresholds: these are but two of the possible approaches. Another just as vital, and one that leads into further depths of experience, *is to attune oneself to motion as expressive gesture,* so that we may learn to read the soul behind it.

We are accustomed to do this with the human face, where the mobile soul-life going on within is at once reflected in the "play" of features. With animals too we read the inner from the outer in their bodily movement. But how much awareness is there of the fact that *everything in Nature has a soul?* that motion is its native language? that it need not remain a book with seven seals to those who, studying its gesture, learn to read it?

Some gesture is obvious, which makes the task a little easier. We commonly recognize the soul in Nature when we use such metaphors as "benign" or "smiling" skies, "biting" cold, "disagreeable" weather, "brooding" mountains; when we speak of the land being "held in the harsh grip" of winter; when we say that a "furious" fire is "raging out of control," that the wind "roars" or "sighs" or "wails" or "whispers," that light "dances" on the water or thunder "growls."

Anthropomorphism on the rampage? Not really, if Nature's soul-life resembles human's — and why should it not, soul being soul wherever we find it? But whatever it may properly be called, it goes at least in the right direction: that of divining feeling behind movement, of conceding inner life to what is so often mistakenly thought of as inanimate.

But we can advance to a subtler sensing by exploring the movement behind seeming stillness. "Holding still," for example, can be intensive motion, an exertion of the will every bit as strenuous as external action. Then too, how much appears still only because it moves so slowly: the growth and withering of living organisms such as trees, vegetation, the bodies of human beings and animals; unseen tides of sap that rise and fall like a mighty breathing; vapors lifting and descending; the slow circling of the seasons.

What a different view of the world dawns upon us when we open ourselves to the soul-life in Nature and begin to live it with her in our sense of movement! To do this deliberately, in willed awareness, is to experience a quickening that knows no end. It leads through door after door, over threshold after threshold, always in the company of fairies, until, as we look back, the landscape we inhabited before begins to seem like the country of the dead and we ourselves wandering in it only half alive.

*   *   *

We think of the seasons as periods of time, and of course they are that. But this is their least interesting aspect. They are also four distinct moods of Nature's soul, four different ways she relates to the interwoven worlds of earth and heaven. Furthermore, each season is, so to speak, a space in time, making four temporal kingdoms over which the four groups of Little People rule.

It is not hard to detect that gnomes are wintry; tradition even paints their nose-tips red. There is a frostiness of mind in them, and a chilly remoteness from others in their rugged individualism. Quartered as they are in depths of earth, theirs is the contractive realm of cold. The very humor to which they are addicted has a sharp, incisive quality. Not only are their jokes always gemlike crystallizations of the drollery of things: they all have "points" which the gnomes quite enjoy watching prick their targets.

There is another aspect to the wintriness of gnomes which must be grasped to understand them. We tend to think that Nature rests in winter because the surface of the earth is still, and, like a sleeper, covered with a blanket. The very opposite is true, however. Beneath our feet fairies have forgathered to live together into the design which Nature has created for the coming year. The most intense activity is going on, comparable to that in human heads when they are absorbed in planning out some creative project. Such thinking is more than ordinarily awake. And that is the state in which we find not just the gnomes, but all the hosts of fairyland in winter.

We live with gnomes when we enter perceptively into winter's gesture. It can be sensed as a holding in, the dynamic that solidifies minerals and makes for the tight cohesion of the frozen earth. We live with undines when we feel with spring, experiencing the upward freeing of the tide of life, letting our own beings flow in waking dream with the undulating and meandering, the surging, swaying and billowing of the fluid element. We live with sylphs when we imagine ourselves moving with the raying light as it suffuses the whole universe in summer, striking into and illumining the outer scene as wisdom the inner. We live with fire-spirits in the mellow warmth that is carried deep into the earth in autumn, when Nature's soul again turns inward, withdrawing the life that poured forth in summer and transmuting it into energy of spirit. Immersing ourselves in this dynamic, we come to understand the ties that link fire-spirits to the life of humans, where they fan creative fires and work in the generating of imaginative vision.

This is to live with Nature where she really lives. Looking behind the scenes, participating more and more sensitively in the action, one begins to wake up to the wonders of the real world where the Little People labor. We grasp what Hamlet may have meant when he admonished the prosaic-souled Horatio, "There are more things in heaven and earth than are dreamt of in your philosophy."

* * *

What a treasure house the earth appears to those who perceive the Middle Kingdom's share in it! Beauty, left as a signature wherever the handiwork of the goddess Nature and of her servitors, the Little People, exists undisturbed: beauty in crystals; in leaves and blossoms; in bird song; in the play of light; in fruit tastes and fragrances; in land- and sea-scapes; in animal forms and their grace of movement; in the mysterious hush of falling snow; in inspired human art; and in more, much more, more beauty than can ever be absorbed or catalogued. Order, that, unlike the dead tidiness of human beings, is throughout a thing of living balance, beautifully wrought and breathing. The dancing rhythm, swift or slow, to be witnessed in evolutionary growth and change through all four kingdoms as movement and stillness intermingle. The power of life surging in wind, wave, fire, in blood of human and beast, in sap's rise and fall, in thought, imagination, feeling, purpose.

And through it all the freshness that is humanity's true food! all the qualities that make us call an experience magical or liken something of the earth to "fairyland."

Yes, close enough to touch with an outstretched hand or the mere lifting of an eyebrow lie the borders of a fabulous country, of that world behind the scenes to which our return is so eagerly awaited by its denizens.